Easy

Origami

Scrapbooking

An Augmented Reality Crafting Experience

by Christopher Harbo

CAPSTONE PRESS

a capstone imprint

First Facts are published by Capstone Press,
1710 Roe Crest Drive, North Mankato, Minnesota 56003
www.mycapstone.com

Library of Congress Cataloging-in-Publication Data
Library of Congress Cataloging-in-Publication data is
available on the Library of Congress website.
ISBN: 978-1-5157-3584-7 (library binding)
ISBN: 978-1-5157-3589-2 (eBook PDF)

Summary: Provides photo-illustrated instructions for making
five origami models and three craft projects. Also includes
embedded video links for online instructional tutorials that
can be accessed with the Capstone 4D app.

Editorial Credits
Sarah Bennett, designer; Laura Manthe, production specialist

The author thanks Rachel Walwood for designing and
creating all of the origami craft projects in this book.

Photo Credits
Photographs and design elements by Capstone Studio: Karon
Dubke, except Shutterstock: BlueOrange Studio, cover, 16
(top left print), 17 (bottom right), Diego Cervo, 10 (two
girls print), 11 (all), MaszaS 16 (bottom print), 17 (bottom
left and top right), oliveromg 22, 23 (all), Pinosub, 16 (top
right print), 17 (top left). Line drawings by Capstone: Sandra
D'Antonio. Additional design elements: Shutterstock: Ammak,
Lena Bukovsky

Printed in the United States of America.
010077S17

Table of Contents

Making Memories Fold by Fold

Folding origami is a great way to make memories with your friends. But using your paper creations to build scrapbook pages can help you capture those memories for a lifetime! With a few photos and some origami finger puppets, you can create a fun, and funny, friendship page. Or perhaps you recently spent a day at the beach with your friends. Showcase it with a stunning under-the-sea page that features paper turtles and whales. No matter which memories you save, origami will help them pop off the scrapbook page!

Download the Capstone 4D App!

Videos for every fold and craft are now at your fingertips with the Capstone 4D app.

To download the Capstone 4D app:
• Search in the Apple App Store or Google Play for "Capstone 4D"
• Click *Install* (Android) or *Get*, then *Install* (Apple)
• Open the application
• Scan any page with this icon

You can also access the additional resources on the web at **www.capstone4D.com** using the password **fold.scraps**

Materials

Origami is great for crafting because the materials don't cost much. Below are the basic supplies you'll use to complete the projects in this book.

origami paper

photos

colored
card stock

scissors

self-adhesive
gemstones

colored paper

double-sided
tape

Terms and Techniques

Folding paper is easier when you understand basic origami folding terms and symbols. Practice the folds below before trying the models in this book.

Valley folds are represented by a dashed line. One side of the paper is folded against the other like a book.

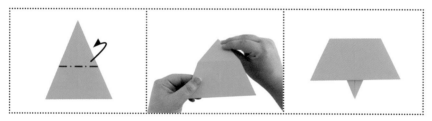

Mountain folds are represented by a dashed and dotted line. The paper is folded sharply behind the model.

Squash folds are formed by lifting one edge of a pocket. The pocket gets folded again so the spine gets flattened. The existing fold lines become new edges.

Inside reverse folds are made by opening a pocket slightly. Then you fold the model inside itself along the fold lines or existing creases.

Outside reverse folds are made by opening a pocket slightly. Then you fold the model outside itself along the fold lines or existing creases.

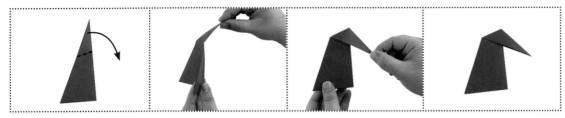

Rabbit ear folds are formed by bringing two edges of a point together using existing fold lines. The new point is folded to one side.

Pleat folds are made by using both a mountain fold and a valley fold.

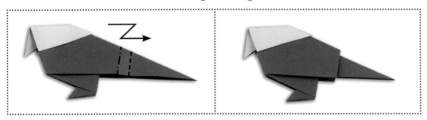

Symbols

Fold the paper in the direction of the arrow.	Fold the paper and then unfold it.	Fold the paper behind.
Turn the paper over, or rotate the paper.	Pleat the paper by reverse folding twice.	Inflate the model by blowing air into it.

Animal Finger Puppets

Tap into your imagination with this simple animal finger puppet. Depending on how you fold the ears, it can look like a cat, a dog, or even a pig.

1 Valley fold corner to corner and unfold.

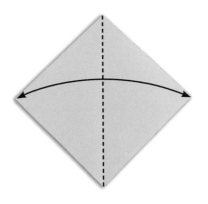

2 Valley fold corner to corner.

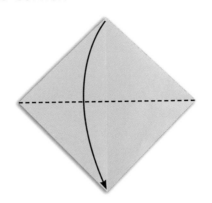

3 Valley fold the points to the corner.

4 Valley fold the top flaps at a slight angle.

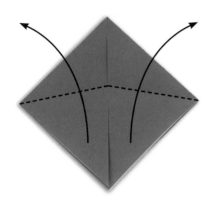

5 Valley fold the top flap. Turn the model over.

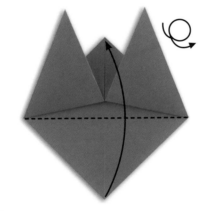

6 Valley fold the corners.

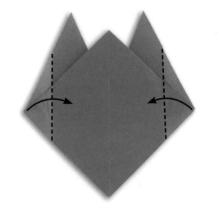

7 Valley fold the corner to the top point.

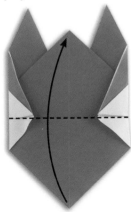

8 Valley fold all layers of the top point. Turn the model over.

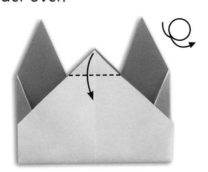

9 Finished animal finger puppet.

Animal Hats Scrapbook Page

A scrapbook page is a great way to remember the good times and goofiness of friendship. Turn origami animal finger puppets into playful hats for your friends.

What You Need

3 photos of your friends

2 or more origami animal finger puppets (hats)

scissors

colored paper

12-inch (30.5-centimeter) square scrapbook page

double-sided tape

*fold finger puppets from 3.5-inch (9-cm) squares

What You Do

1 Pick one photo for the animal hats. It should show people who are large enough for the hats to fit them well.

2 Trim around the edges of the people in the photo you've selected. Set aside.

3 Cut colored paper into strips and rectangles that are slightly larger than the photos. Also cut out letters to spell words such as "FRIENDS" or "CLASSMATES."

4 Arrange your photos on the scrapbook page in a way that pleases you. Use the paper strips and rectangles as decorations and borders behind the photos. Place any words you cut out wherever they look best.

5 When everything is where you want it, tape all of the photos, borders, decorations, and letters in place on the scrapbook page.

6 Place the animal hats on top of the photos of the friends you trimmed around in step 2. Tape the hats in place to finish your friendship page.

Whale

Thar she blows! Blue whales are giants of the sea. Make your paper versions large or small in any color you like.

1 Valley fold corner to corner in both directions and unfold.

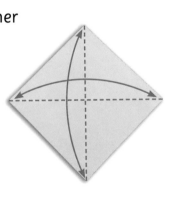

2 Valley fold the edges to the center and unfold.

3 Valley fold the edges to the center and unfold.

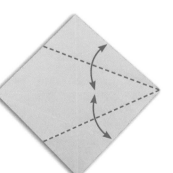

4 Rabbit ear fold on the existing creases.

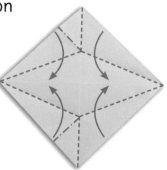

5 Turn the model over.

6 Valley fold the point to the center crease.

7 Valley fold the top and bottom points part way to the center.

8 Valley fold the model in half.

9 Valley fold the flap. Repeat behind.

10 Cut the point in half. Valley fold both tips of the tail.

11 Valley fold the top layer of the tail.

12 Finished whale.

⭐ Turtle

As soon as they hatch, baby sea turtles scamper across the beach and into the ocean. Fold dozens of tiny turtles to create your own race to the waves.

1 Valley fold corner to corner in both directions and unfold. Turn the paper over.

2 Valley fold edge to edge and unfold.

3 Valley fold edge to edge.

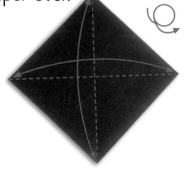

4 Squash fold.

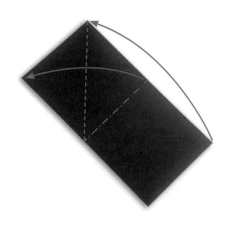

5 Valley fold the top flaps to the center and unfold. Repeat behind.

6 Inside reverse fold the top flaps. Repeat behind.

7 Valley fold the top flap. Repeat behind.

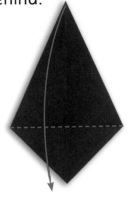

8 Valley fold the top flap's point.

9 Valley fold the point.

10 Valley fold the point.

11 Valley fold the top flap on the existing crease.

12 Inside reverse fold the top points to make front legs.

13 Turn the model over.

14 Valley fold the top flap on the existing crease.

15 Valley fold the top flap.

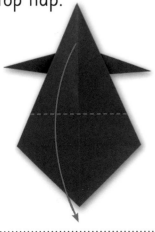

16 Cut the top flap's point in half. Valley fold the two flaps to create the back legs. Turn the model over.

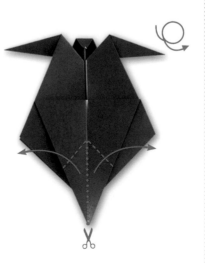

17 Finished turtle.

Under-the-Sea Scrapbook Page

Save the memories of your latest trip to the beach with an under-the-sea scrapbook page. Origami whales and turtles will help you capture the fun above and below the water.

What You Need

3 or more photos

12-inch (30.5-cm) square scrapbook page

scissors

colored paper

origami whale

3 small origami turtles

double-sided tape

self-adhesive gemstones

What You Do

1 Arrange the photos on the scrapbook page in a way that pleases you. If necessary, cut off any photo edges that have people or scenery you don't want to see.

2 Cut colored paper into strips and rectangles that are slightly larger than the photos. Place them behind the photos as borders.

3 Arrange the whale and turtles so they look like they are swimming around the photos.

4 When everything is where you want it, tape all of the photos, borders, and origami in place.

5 Stick gemstones around the page to give your underwater scene a little extra sparkle.

*fold the whale from a 6-inch (15-cm) square and the turtles from 2- to 4-inch (5- to 10-cm) squares

Cornflower

Cornflowers burst like stars into brilliant shades of light blue. With four points bursting outward, this origami blossom looks great in any color.

1 Valley fold corner to corner in both directions and unfold. Turn the paper over.

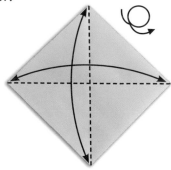

2 Valley fold edge to edge and unfold.

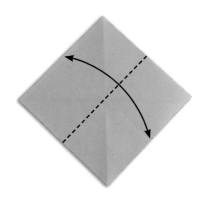

3 Valley fold edge to edge.

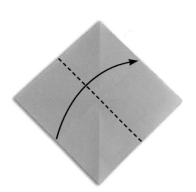

4 Squash fold.

5 Valley fold the top flaps to the center and unfold. Repeat behind.

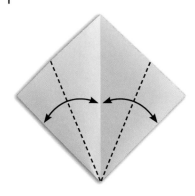

6 Squash fold on the creases made in step 5. Repeat behind.

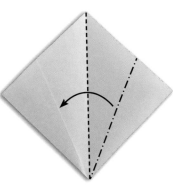

7 Valley fold the top flap. Repeat behind.

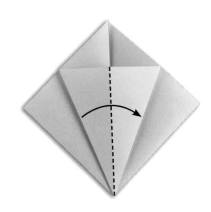

8 Squash fold. Repeat behind.

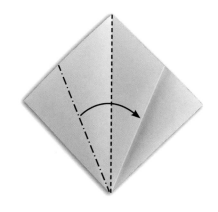

9 Valley fold the top layer while squash folding the inside points.

10 Squash fold the points to form petals.

11 Finished cornflower.

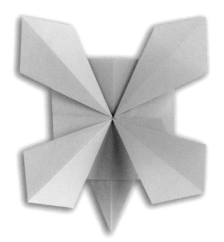

Floral Scrapbook Page

A simple floral-themed scrapbook page is the perfect way to capture a summer picnic in the park. Make paper leaves to serve as frames for your photos. Then add a few origami blossoms for just the right burst of color.

What You Need

scissors

3 or more photos

2 8.5- by 11-inch (22- by 28-cm) sheets of green paper

12-inch (30.5-cm) square scrapbook page

origami cornflower

2 origami camellias

double-sided tape

*fold all origami flowers from 6-inch (15-cm) squares

What You Do

1 Cut curves around opposite corners of the photos to shape each one like a leaf.

2 Place the photos on the green paper. Cut around the photos, leaving a little extra room on all sides, to make slightly larger leaf shapes. These leaves will serve as frames for your photos.

3 Arrange the photos and leaves on the scrapbook page in a way that pleases you.

4 Place one origami flower near each photo.

5 Cut long, thin strips of green paper to serve as stems. Arrange the stems so they connect to the flowers and leaves.

6 When everything is where you want it, tape all of the photos, leaves, stems, and origami in place.

7 Trim off the ends of any stems that meet the edges of the scrapbook page to complete the craft.

Read More

Bolte, Mari. *Colorful Creations: You Can Make and Share.* Sleepover Girls Crafts. North Mankato, Minn.: Capstone Press, 2015.

Formaro, Amanda. *Paper Mania: Crafts, Activities, Facts, and Fun.* White Plains, N.Y.: Studio Fun Books, 2015.

Song, Sok. *Everyday Origami: A Foldable Fashion Guide.* Fashion Origami. North Mankato, Minn.: Capstone Press, 2016.

Turnbull, Stephanie. *Paper Crafts.* Try This! Mankato, Minn.: Smart Apple Media, 2016.

Internet Sites

FactHound offers a safe, fun way to find Internet sites related to this book. All of the sites on FactHound have been researched by our staff.

Here's all you do:
Visit *www.facthound.com*
Type in this code: 9781515735847